# LETTERS OF JULIET

# TO THE KNIGHT IN

# RUSTY ARMOR

J.D. GILL

KDP

2024

One quiet afternoon Ramakrishna beheld a beautiful woman ascend from the Ganges and approach the grove in which he was meditating. He perceived that she was about to give birth to a child. In a moment the babe was born, and she gently nursed it. Presently, however, she assumed a horrible aspect, took the infant in her now ugly jaws and crushed it, chewed it. Swallowing it, she returned again the Ganges, where she disappeared.

--The Gospel of Sri Ramakrishna

# CONTENTS

# INTRODUCTORY NOTE

Written in 1993, these letters are intended to be a companion piece read in conjunction with *The Knight in Rusty Armor* by Robert Fisher. They seek to fill in Juliet's side of the equation. Read together, these works provide for reflection on interior realizations that are essential in relationships.

At the suggestion of Dr. Brad Reedy these letters have been issued in stand alone form for easier access.

## LETTER ONE

Dear Sir:

Ever since you saw fit to leave your son and me so you wouldn't have to take off that ridiculous armor you love so much, I have been trying to pick up the pieces of my life.

At first I was furious with you. Like those glamour boys of my youth, you too had vanished at the simple request I made of you. Perhaps it was asking too much? Your son Christopher, doesn't even know you--but he longs for you anyway! Hopefully HE will grow up to be the kind of person who will think beyond himself!

My friends from the neighboring castles were quick to agree with me, and you may be sure, you will probably have a tough time of it when, or if, you return to these parts.

Still, since you have been gone, my feelings swing back and forth. At first as I said,

I was so angry with you for just going off--
in a way, I still am!   But then, I realized I
needed to figure out what I was going to do
now.

As time passed, I began to convince myself I was better off with you gone, though I
never was much one for being alone.   I in-
vited in all sorts of house guests, and had the
castle redone in tasteful, stylish banners
rather than that stuff you were always so
fond of.

My mother came to stay, but your son only
cried and was very cold to her, I must say--
the apple doesn't fall far from the tree.   I
tried to comfort him, but he would always
test the limits and end up hurting everyone's
feelings. Perhaps it is a male trait.

After mother left, Sir Geoffrey, our neigh-
bor whose wife died in childbirth two years
ago--remember--began to pass the evenings
with us. I think he was taken with me, and I
confess I began to think of having an affair
with him. He thoughtfully brought baubles
and small casks of wine. Once, even, when
he was leaving, he grabbed me and kissed
me. I nearly lost my breath, it had been so
long since you and I had made love, but I
was confused and pushed him away.   Like

the rest of you, he went off that night and hasn't been around since.

As I said, my life by myself has been quite full, though Christopher is a bit hard to manage. Yet, no matter what I do, I am tormented by my thoughts for you. Damn you! Why is it so difficult--why is the calm I want always eluding me?

I can't decide what to do. My friends tell me to forget you and get on with my life. But I keep remembering little things about you; times we shared when we were happy, when life was full and wonderful. I remember bathing with you in that forest pool, how you held me, and how good I felt.

Little by little, I have begun missing you more even though I hate you--and wonder where did our love go?

I tried putting your picture back up but couldn't keep it there. Again, I decided to go on without you. I thought of leaving the country and moving to the city. I couldn't do it though.

Christopher is so sad. Nothing consoles him. He isn't eating well, and he even let his pet falcon get away! If he doesn't snap out of it soon, he will never be a knight himself. Last week his tutor left him in disgust. "Teach him to sew!" he said!

So, after much thought I have decided to try to find you. Maybe we can talk. I have to settle this once and for all. I don't know where you are, though I have been told you went back into the woods. I am terribly afraid of those woods, as you know, but I want to find you and see if you really are as impossible and closed as I remember--or did I just invent it?

Sometimes I think you must need me. Last week I dreamed you were dead, and it frightened me. Anyway, I must find a way to solve this and get on with my life. I hate feeling this way.

I've taken Christopher to stay for a short time with my younger sister Isabella in the next valley. He can play with his cousin there, and they can go to school together. He is getting quite big now. He doesn't want me to go, but I explained how it was important, and he waved to me when I left.

If you return home while I'm still gone, send me a letter. The bishop will know where I am, and I will remain faithful in my church attendance, so someone will let me know you are home.

I hope you are well and we can work this mess out soon.

Regards,

Juliet

# LETTER TWO

My Dear Knight:

In the time since I met Marithe, so much has changed!  I scarcely know my name.  I can't believe a viewpoint can change so much!

After I left the castle; I must say I did not have an easy time.  It was harder than I imagined being away from Christopher.  Many days I thought the longing I had for him would tear me apart and put an end to my crazy journey--for I got lost and crazy indeed in the woods.  It was hard finding traces of you.  I don't know how you do it, going in there all the time.

My friends urged me not to go.  They don't like you anyway.  They wanted to plan a summer's feast, and I often wished I had listened to them.  My paths were paths of futility.  I got lost no matter where I went.  The sounds of the woods scared me, and I doubted I would ever survive. I got hungry and sick. I developed a strange taste for water, but this was not easy to find, especially those streams from the heights, fed by winter snows.

I fell into despair. I couldn't find my way back, or I would have gone, immediately. I was lost and terrified! I don't know if you have ever felt this feeling or not, but it is awful--I could not imagine continuing anywhere. My life seemed a long series of failures; every impulse I felt had been futile.

I fell by the side of a mountain meadow where I knew I would die. I sobbed and sobbed for Christopher, for my friends, my mother and father (the Duke and Duchess), and for my older sisters I had not seen in so many years. I even sobbed for you and for the failure our dreams have been.

As I was lying there, the strangest thing happened. A woman--I am still not certain whether or not she was an apparition--appeared beside me, a strange soft light around her. The light was white and pale blue.

"Who are you?" I asked amazed.

"I am Marithe," she replied, "take a drink from my cup."

She held out a silver cup with the sweetest tasting water. It seemed to heal my weariness all at once, and I sat up.

"Stop staring--you can come with me," she said and helped me to my feet. Her light almost seemed to cover me too--and I swear it mended my smock and healed the scratches the branches had cut into my arms, legs, and face. It even brushed my hair.

"But who are you," I insisted.

"I am the woman of the woods," she said, "and I have come to you in a form you can comprehend."

"Don't be afraid, come; I can help you find what you want so you can discover your way home."

"You know the way home?" I stammered.

"Come child," she said, "I have a lot to tell you."

With that she helped me up and led me across the grass to a place just beyond the clearing where she had a strange, open house. It kept looking like a temple with pillars, but then it was a roof on poles.

Whatever it was, it was enchanted, and I feared for my life. A dreary death of misery is to be preferred, I thought, to some diabolical end at the hands of evil spirits.

I decided to run away. (Actually I decided this almost every day I was with Marithe.) She read my thoughts and quieted me with an unbelievable calm. Her presence filled me, and I could only wonder what lay ahead for me.

"Come, sit on the pillows," she said. "I want to tell you something."

When I sat down, Marithe poured out a glass of crystal water for me and said, "You are well aware of the knight's armor; are you also aware of your own?"

"I sometimes wish I had some," I replied.

"Oh, you have some--and it is perhaps greater--but at least more dangerous--than the knight's."

I was a bit insulted by these words, but de-cided to listen more.

"So tell me, what is my armor," I said.

"What do you think?" she insisted.

"I don't know, perhaps my nosiness?" I said.

"No, not that," she said.

"I don't know what it is; what is it, my worry?" I asked.

"Your anger is your armor," was her reply.

"My anger!" I was astounded. "I don't see myself as angry," I stressed.

"I know," said Marithe, "and that is part of the problem." "You see everyone's armor but your own."

"Your anger covers up your fear."

"Think back," she said, "to when you gave your knight your demand--either you take off that armor or I will take the child and leave, you said."

"He deserved it; he was ignoring me!" I shouted.

"I rest my case" said Marithe.

"What if he had said, 'Get rid of your anger or I will take the child and leave?'"

"I would have told him to take a royal hike!" I ex-claimed.

"Well, can you hear it yet" my patient friend said with an almost eerie grin.

I had to admit, the idea began to have some weight with me, though I had never considered it before.

Somehow she was weaving some magic or something, because ordinarily I would have fought for my own position.

Now, strangely I didn't feel like it. I almost wanted to try something new.

I confess, I had never thought of myself as being especially angry before. I just thought of the world as sadly out of balance, tilting in an unfair way.

Yet, as she talked, I thought maybe it was true. Maybe it was true I had been stuck on myself and had been so busy trying to make my own life work, I had gotten lost in myself. Maybe this is how I have been with you too and just demanded you give up your armor and please me without thinking what that would mean to you. Still, I must say I have always been raised to think one did the right thing, regardless of how one felt.

What strange thoughts these were!

I sat up late into the night all alone thinking how my parents never did ask me how I felt about anything--they only pushed me to get it right. And since I had been raised with one right way, I may have been quite innocently trying to shape you up accordingly.

In the morning I woke up with an unnerved feeling. I found Marithe by the stream in deep meditation.

When she had finished, I asked her, "How do I get this problem resolved?"

"You are a quick learner," she said. "You must find a way to get beyond your anger. This requires you to get it out, look at it straightaway, and then move through it.

Most people simply deny they have it or try to avoid it."

"How do I do this?" I asked.

"The first step is to let go of your crusades, your expectations, your endless trying to make your life work, to get rid of your fear, your successes in the social club--and simply sit with yourself, alone, so your true life can find a way to contact you."

"My true life?" I asked.

"The one you discover within you, rather than the one you construct outside by your own efforts," she replied.

"Just sit with myself?" I asked.

"Just sit--here by the steam," she said.

"How long will this take?"

"Until the waters are able to give you a true reflection," she said gently.

Then she slipped away into her white and blue light--and then the light diffused through the wood and across the top of the stream.

I was terrified. Alone. I still didn't know where I was--why hadn't I asked her?--and I ached for Christopher.

I fell to the ground and began to weep. I cried all day and all night. I have never cried so much before. The anguish of my life came out in my tears. I was touched in a way I never expected--in a way my mother and friends had taught me to fear.

I saw it was true; deep down, beneath it all, I feared everything.

My old life closed.

Did Marithe see me clearly enough to help me find who I really am?

After a day or so, I decided to trust her. I decided to sit by the stream and see what happened.

This is my plan if I can go through with it; it is what I am going to do now. I am worried about this whole business--it seems so strange--but I don't know what else to do.

If a messenger comes by, I will give him this letter. If you receive it, please know I will try to be home soon. My absence from our son stabs at my heart--I love him so.


Love,


Juliet

## LETTER THREE

My Dearest Knight:

I am writing to you through my tears. I have cried so much I don't know who I am anymore. One thing is sure, I am not who I thought I was when I tried to live by my own efforts.

I have found I love you so.

After Marithe left me here, I wandered back and forth aimlessly for days. Demons kept chasing me, urgencies pressed in on me. I kept getting caught in scenes from my past.

I even began to feel my mother, poor woman, had been my warden! Yes. She kept me from being myself and forced me, again and again, to fit in. My school friends and the ladies of the castle each agreed. Ours was a difficult lot they said, only by sticking together could we find real support

in our alien world. I would have done anything they asked just to keep from being
kicked out of the club.

I can now see I never should have listened
to them. I joined their club instead of join-
ing life.

I'm afraid I have lost you, because I tried
to force you to join that club too--agree with
it.

I hope I haven't crippled our son.

My tears are endless. I didn't know anything before.

I have been sitting still, hour after hour--
and have sunk further into my quiet.

In this state, away from familiar places, I
have found every once in a while, notes left
by Marithe--though I didn't see her all this
time.

The first note simply said: "WHAT MAT-
TERS?"

I thought about this for a long while, and
each time, my list changed.

Birds came to watch with me. The ants, the grasses seemed to join with me.

Suddenly, one day, I saw life laid out all about me, like the air I was breathing. I realized it was life itself that mattered. Simply life itself. Christopher and you.

I saw it all around me. It was just clearly there. And I began to see that it was part of me, I was part of it--I *was* it somehow--it was me.

I began to feel I wasn't me; I was life. I had no separate space, no single shadow.

I thought, "What can I give to life?"

And when I had this thought, I also knew the answer.

Life needed me to support it. You need me to support you. Christopher needs me to support him.

Nothing needs me to rearrange it, shape it up to my own advantage, triumph over it.

No, life needed my hands to hold it up, to be with it.

I began to feel I had turned into part of the very stream.

I just wanted to give things, be things, be asked.

I wanted to embrace the trees in my madness.

And I thought of home.

Then I found another note which asked: "WHAT IS THE DANGER?"

I could imagine all sorts of dangers, but I grew confused at my thoughts and could not answer the question.

Day after day I sat by the stream, watching it dance in the sunlight, in the moonlight. I watched the earth in its richness like an open hand--and I wanted to be like that earth myself, the field that holds up life, upon which life depends.

After a while it came to me, nothing IN this place had final control--was able to control life. There was no real power but the thread of life itself within, behind it all.

Could that be the answer, I thought. Could the answer be to stop wishing for power and control oneself? Stop being individual?

Power and control is foreign and imposed, I thought. The fields don't work this way. They simply have the measure that is given them. Is this their message?

Does life work this way too?

Was that my great error? Had I been forever lost in trying to arrange my life my way--to make it turn out the way I wanted--so my own dreams would come true--so I had not seen life had more important things to do than pay attention to *my* dreams? And weren't my dreams my attempt to be something or somewhere I was not, rather than accepting what or where I was?

Had I, in short, been abusive to life rather than loving? Had I forgotten to accept it, surrender to it, and thank it for its beauty? Had I not, rather, been demanding of it, determined to change it, scarred by my attempts at control--control of that which only life can ever control?

Have I treated you this way?

I realized the things of the field were not really trying to win—but just to be there and stay alive. They lived the lives they were destined to live--either advantageous or not--and the whole fabric was therefore made beautiful.

Is that our message, my husband? Do we need to find that we too are part of the field and stop wanting things to be different, stop selfishly disrupting the whole? Do we not need to believe that what is parceled out for us is ours already if we will only accept it and make ourselves available to it?

And what is parceled out for me does not take away from what is parceled out for you.

I came to think this is the message.

Then I realized what has happened between us. I saw your armor was in the way, but I did not see my expectations were in the way just the same. My anger at you when you wouldn't do what I wanted left you out as surely as your armor left me out.

Was this part of the reason you turned more and more to your own armor anyway?

Was it the reason I turned?

The pain in my heart about this made me see I had discovered the danger.

I realized what we do to stay safe wounds others.

That night I had a dream. I was summoned to the GREAT HALL OF WOMEN. There, I was led before a large group of women, all of whom began shrieking at me for my betrayal of them. They accused me of abandoning my pledge to keep them first.

They humiliated me, degraded me, and promised to make my life miserable if I did not leave you--in my heart--forever. They harangued me while they told me to "think it over."

I was torn by this demand and terrified to think I had to choose between you and them. I resigned myself, however, as I have done so many times--and began to let you go.

But I thought suddenly of those tender times between us, that night in the forest and your sweet hands. Such tenderness I have not known anywhere else--even its memory made me drunk with desire for you--even if you are impossible!

The unthinkable began to occur to me: I would leave *them*. I sobbed in an uncontrollable attempt to cleanse my whole life.

When I awoke, I was exhausted, yet in this state I realized Marithe too had openly reached out to me. Much differently from the voices in my dream, she had helped me without asking for return.

It came to me with great force: love is not so much a getting together and making dreams work as it is using your energy to help life get where it needs to get.

I knew Marithe had been right.

My knight, I have done so poorly with my great love for you; can you forgive me?

I have done poorly with Christopher.

(At this point, I imagined Marithe's voice saying I had done poorly with *me*.)

Where was Marithe? I wanted to ask her why the women in the Hall had been raised to fit in rather than being true to themselves. Why were we, each of us, taught the notions we had been taught about being "correct," when these exact notions ensured our failure in the world?

As the morning wore on and silver lifted in the trees, the surrounding meadow settled into its life of the day. I was completely at the mercy of my thoughts, which were flooding me with great urgency.

My realizations about love had disoriented me, and I began to think of the heart as its own country.

Had I focused so much on outcomes, I had ignored the land of feelings, which is complete in itself?

My muscles relaxed. I felt no will to move.

The heart has its feelings regardless of the outcomes. Being true to these feelings is the thing.

My thoughts shifted from the earth to the sky.

What about that great region that is made from only seeing--rather than possessing?

I had spent all my life on the ground, because I had been taught by my mother, sisters, everyone, that the ground was the "real" place. Suddenly, I wasn't so sure.

My knight, I saw your place, which is also beyond the ground. I saw where you had lived, had been trying to teach me. I wanted to explore your country with you--I had always feared it before.

Life is both, isn't it?

Perhaps you were afraid I would require you to sacrifice the air for the ground. I was afraid to leave the ground.

I understood what your armor was for--and I understood what my anger was for.

Marithe came and embraced me. Somehow I had not been embraced like this before. I felt very much at home for the first time and let go to silence.

Evening was beginning to fall. "There is one journey left," she said, but I was too drained to pay much attention.

If you get my letter, please hear what I have said. I long to see you again, for your embrace…but I also, with all my heart, wish you well on your journey.

All my love,

Juliet

## LETTER FOUR

My Darling:

After my realizations about love, I felt my whole life open, that I could no longer stay away from the call of life, of you, our son-- these longings in the fullest measure.

Whether she truly understood this or not, I don't know, but Marithe took me floating with her on her light.

I drifted with her though houses of dying children, of poor people wracked with pain.

I saw eyes grateful for rags and broken things. I saw them pass each other and touch, imploring.

I heard them, and their heaviness was within me.

We passed gatherings of the cruel and parties at the best castles.

We passed people with their lives in their hands, moving through grey, ordinary days.

A feeling I cannot name twisted in my openness, and I realized I must devote my life to save my life.

I no longer wanted to succeed or be on top of anything. I did not want applause.

I wanted to be necessary to life, to your life, to our son's life, to all life.

Love really is a giving rather than a getting, but so much comes back!

Somehow, I can't stop weeping. I am not the wife, the mother, the friend I was before. I have been lifted.

I have wept waves of tears for me, for you, for Christopher—and now I am ready to wait with life for what life wants.

What do you want, my dear knight?

I have practiced saying "yes" and realize I must go on without reassurance.

It was so hard for me, dear knight, to admit I had brought others what I wanted, not what they wanted. I called this "caring" or "nurturing" before.

Oh, have I done anything right?

Marithe led me across a great river. It was slow like the motion of death. Death was all around us.

She is leading me to my death, I thought with a sudden terror--and I froze with fear.

But her steady hand was like your hand, and through yet more tears I found myself letting go. I let go and let go. I let go until I no longer was. Death was a kind of ultimate moment of love for me. I let go to death's time.

I truly felt it: time was the lover calling for me! To be lifted and consumed in such love! To be made part of all that could be! Through almost panic I went forward.

And then--I couldn't believe it--I let go of her hand and drifted by myself. I crossed the river as if it were the ground. I passed the up-stretched hands of the suffering penitents. I approached the spring of dark water at the center.

Without a thought, as if my body could not have done otherwise, I bent and drank in the liquid of time. No words could describe my sensations.

I saw what it meant. The answer is to not to want or need anything that does not rise out of one's truth. Since we are life, my dear knight, what do we really want or need?

We cannot live because we cannot get beyond our wants and needs. That is what love is trying to teach us.

We hear so little.

I saw my anger had been in the way of my letting go. It is truly armor, my knight. It kept me too closed in.

For the first time in my life I felt free and realized how lucky I was that my dreams had *not* worked.

What surprise to feel Marithe's hand on my arm. She embraced me with the same emotion as the water. We were truly one in that embrace. I knew what she knew.

As she held me, I softened. I found myself yielding to her embrace. I could not help thinking back to you and the embraces we once had. My thoughts were scattered, trying to grasp the great meaning of yielding to an embrace, how it centers, how it reminds, how it lifts.

I found my thoughts returning again and again to you. Marithe was reminding me my love for time needed focus--the embrace of time wakens most fully, I thought, in the focus of a real lover's embrace. One let go *through* such an embrace to time. The embraces fuse.

Marithe could not stay with me in this way, and I longed for you. What would we be like *without* our armor, my knight?

Thoughts of such encounters gripped me while I lay back in Marithe's arms. I know she understood.

I felt again the way I felt when we were first lovers all those years ago in the roses, remember? I was again drunk with birth; I was drunk with eternity, whom I want to say owns me.

The sky darkened. We walked back along the path as sisters, Marithe and I--more than sisters. We walked as part of the water, as its spray.

When we were in the forest again at Marithe's little temple, I felt so full I could not speak.

For the first time, I dropped to my knees and felt myself ready. I felt my life in my body. I felt my heart in its own season.

After a long time, Marithe said, "You will be leaving now?"

I nodded.

"I will walk with you," she said. "We will leave when you are ready."

If you are home to receive this letter, my dear knight, I will be back soon. I hope you can accept me. If you are not home, I will save the letter to show you where I have been since you have been gone.

My knight, I am quieter.

I wish you the trembling of new leaves in summer.

I wish you rain.

I wish you the laughter of your son.

I wish you all my heart--which is my life.

Dark blood on the rose.

Dark tears on the sunrise.

Dark peace in the stillness.

Dark stillness in the sunrise.

Dark sunrise in the dark time and in the great light.

My love, my love, my love,

Juliet

# COMPARISON OF THEMES IN THE KNIGHT IN RUSTY ARMOR AND JULI-ET'S LETTERS

| ISSUE | KNIGHT | JULIET |
|---|---|---|
| Part of Self | Masculine Side | Feminine Side |
| Quest | To light | To life |
| Where | Outside | Inside |
| Guide | Merlin | Marithe |
| Armor | Control with force | Control with anger and withdrawal |
| Lessons | Silence (inner self) | Move beyond conformity |
| | Face fear | Abandon control (will) |
| Moral | | |

1) To become whole, we must experience each other's region.

2) We must move beyond a specific context.

# NOTE ON METAPHOR AND MYTH

It is no accident that for thousands of years, the essential topic of human mythology has concerned a journey. This journey is to discover a true realization of the genuine self in accord with the greater (i.e., more expanded) truths of reality.

It is also easy to see that everything we do is limited to some extent by the fact we can only have a partial, or limited, point of view. This is true of ourselves and also the world in which we live (that is, we can't have every experience and perspective--we can't know everything*).*

Also, there is always a difference between being *inside* some perspective, point of view, or experience, and being *outside* that same perspective, point of view, or experience. For this reason, an inside and an outside view will rarely, if ever, be the same.

Consider: when we grew up, we were taught and we typically learned to fit into the rules and views of our particular families and peer groups. This training determined among other things what approved conduct was, what "reality" was, who we were, who others were, what life was about, &c. Mastering this code enabled us to avoid most of the family or group zaps--and we were thus able to communicate with and become an approved part of the "rhythm" of the family or group unit.

Armed with this code which we had mastered, we eventually ventured out into the world--where we found much to our dismay the code did not work as well.

The reason for this is simple. The world is multidimensional in nature, and we each come from a single or limited experience.

Because of this limitation, we are constantly being confronted with situations in which the training we have learned does not work. At this point, we often have a problem.

What we typically try to do when we are confronted with something--or especially someone--who does't follow our codes is to convert them to the "proper code" (which is, of course, our own code). May the best code win.

When we have some alone time, we may turn inward. Who am I "really?" we may ask. We find it is a hard question to answer.

If we continue in this enterprise, we begin to discover the self we find by a process of direct discovery or our own immediate experience, is typically a very different self from the self we are taught we are to be by family (or "social") codes.

(A patient of mine said, "I don't know who that was in my childhood, but it wasn't me.")

Myths speak to the immediately discovered self instead of the taught self.

This is why myths resonate in us when we hear them. Descriptions, on the other hand, typically tell us something new (i.e., teachings). Myths resonate within us as the dimensions revealed in the myth are also dimensions which are (metaphorically) alive in us (though often dormant).

For thousands of years, the essential theme of human mythology has been an attempt to pursue an expanded realization of the real self in accord with greater truths of reality-- rather than remaining held in a view that is in accord with the perceptions and experiences of one's specific parents or group.

The "journey" of mythology is a metaphor.

Linguistically, descriptions involve a factual use of language. Metaphors, on the other hand, involve an evocative use.

Thus metaphors seek to create a *direct* emotional experience or connection. For this reason, metaphors are ideally suited to the feeling life. And, in this way, metaphors *always* suggest an expansion beyond a simple descriptive view--to a more expanded context, if you will.

A metaphor is a figure of speech in which elements are equated in a symbolic or evocative way. It might be said metaphorical language evokes an emotion in the heart (which is a metaphor).

Metaphors may be said to have a denotation and a connotation. The denotation is always some physical thing, but the connotation always involves an emotion of some sort.

It is in this way metaphor functions as a device to link the external, descriptive world to the direct emotions or the heart.

We might say description is the language of the head. Metaphor is the language of the emotional experience.

Without the development of metaphor, human history would only be a collection of facts--however accurately reported. We would only have history.

With metaphor, we additionally have mythology, religion and--perhaps above all--poetry.

In Greece, the one who had access to the gods was not the priest, but the poet. The priests were considered to be functionaries (and that is what most of them are to this day).

Joseph Campbell said the only person who can keep a mythology alive is the artist. That is his job; the mythology making of the environment.

Metaphor and metaphorical thinking is the technique that allows us to move beyond the world of facts (or the lower forms) and contact the world beyond (the higher forms).

Actually, in one way or another, each of us has been involved in this search beyond--or behind—the appearances of our lives to find a greater truth--the truth of what our lives may actually be about in the "big picture."

Anyone who has studied literature in much depth knows that great literature has dealt over and over with the essential human truths and themes.

Art is again, in fact, the effective link between the world we know and the world which lies beyond—par excellence.

Religion, too, in its ancient form was "alive."

It is a fundamental truth from early myths —as reflected, for example, in the Vedas, the ancient Hindu texts, that what we don't know always surrounds and supports what we do know.

This is the ground. It is the "out-there" and thus every human being--every one of us--must come to some sort of terms with what is "out there," what is "beyond."

As I have said, this "wider" level of life is accessed through the use of metaphor.

It is the larger life that heals the smaller life.

See also: Campbell, J. Hero With a Thousand Faces (1949), and The Inner Reaches of Outer Space (1988); Eliade, M. The Sacred and the Profane (1957), and Myth and Reality (1963).

# ABOUT THE AUTHOR

J.D. Gill is a clinical psychologist at the University of Utah. She is an Adjunct Associate Professor of Psychology, a Clinical Professor of Counseling Psychology, and an Adjunct Associate Professor of Psychiatry in the University of Utah School of Medicine. Dr. Gill maintains a busy practice at the University of Utah.

Dr. Gill has degrees in English Literature, Philosophy, Psychology, and two post docs in psychoanalytic psychotherapy. She studied in the Writing Program at the University of Utah. She has been a practicing psychologist for over fifty years and has presented over five hundred seminars, lectures, workshops, and papers. A world traveler, Dr. Gill has actively sought to experience multiple viewpoints and perspectives.

NOTES:

Made in United States
Troutdale, OR
03/19/2024

18576166R00037